DOGS

MIXED PICROSS VOL 1

Mixed Dogs Themed Logic Puzzles

Picross - Griddler - Nonogram - Hanjie

Quipoppe Publications

Easy

Puzzle 1 - solution on page: 55

3
4
4
4
4
5
6
7
8
8
8
9
9
2 6
2 6
2 7
1 5 8

1 | 8 1 | 16 | 14 | 12 1 | 9 1 | 11 | 10 | 9 | 7 | 5 | 2 | 2 | 1 | 1 | 1 | 1 | 1 | 1 | 1

Puzzle 2 - solution on page: 55

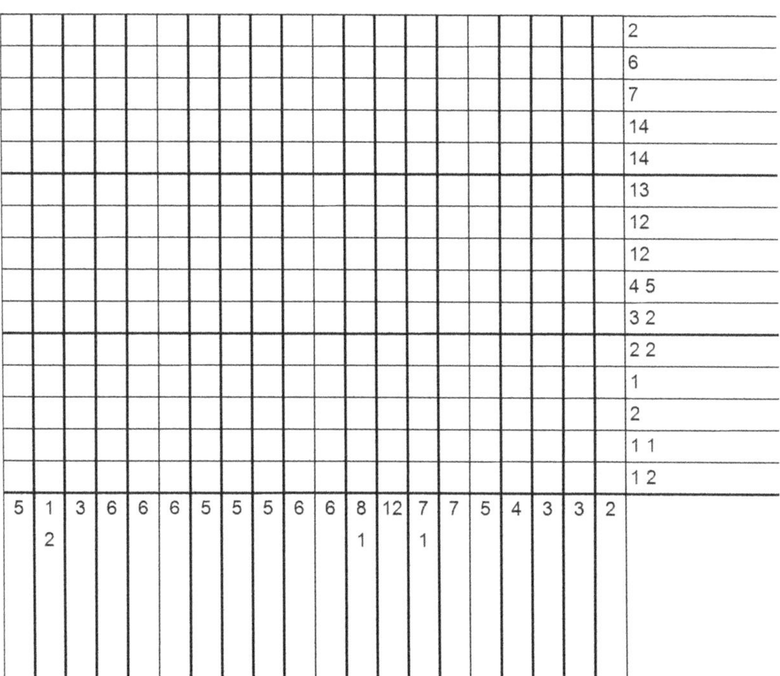

Puzzle 3 - solution on page: 57

Row clues: 3 | 4 | 6 | 7 | 8 | 11 | 12 | 13 | 13 | 13 | 5 4 | 4 2 | 5 3 | 1 2 2 | 1 2 2 | 1 1 1 | 1 2 | 1 | 1

Column clues: 2 | 2 | 2 | 6 3 | 9 2 | 9 | 8 | 6 | 5 | 6 | 6 | 7 | 7 3 | 14 | 11 1 | 9 | 4 | 3 | 3 | 2

Puzzle 4 - solution on page: 57

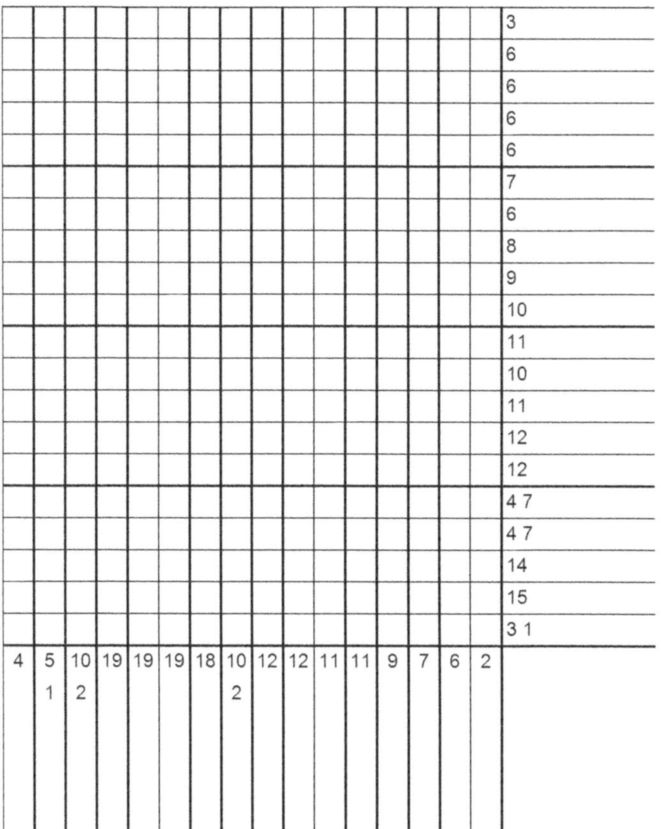

Medium

Puzzle 5 - solution on page: 59

3
9
11
10
11 12
28
28
28
28
28
26
26
24
24
24
5 14
4 10
4 7
3 6
3 6
3 6
2 6
3 6
4 8
4 5
4

3	7	16	20	21	14	12	11	11	11	11	12	12	12	11	12	12	13	21	24	24	25	25	23	17	14	11	9	9	2
					3	2	1																	1	1				

Puzzle 6 - solution on page: 61

Row clues:

1
1
2
4
5
8
7
4
7
18
20
20
19
19
4 9
5 7
4 2
4 2
4 2
3 2
1 1 2
1 2 2
2
3
1 2
2
1

Column clues:

3	3	2	5	4	9	8	8	7	5	5	5	5	5	5	6	7	7	8	8	8	17	22	12	10	6	4	3	2	1
	1			1																			3						

Puzzle 7 - solution on page: 63

Column clues:

1	2	3	4	5	6	7	8	9	10	11	12	13	14	15	16	17	18	19	20	21	22	23	24	25	26	27	28	29
2	5	6	29	29	21	21	29	29	5	3	16	14	16	15	13	12	11	9	7	2	2	1	2	1	1	1	1	
	2	12			1	3			19	18																		

Row clues:

Row	Clue
1	5
2	7
3	9
4	10
5	10
6	10
7	9
8	6
9	6
10	8
11	9
12	10
13	10
14	12
15	13
16	14
17	15
18	15
19	16
20	16
21	17
22	16
23	2 13
24	2 13
25	2 13
26	2 14
27	2 15
28	2 5 7 3
29	2 3 7 5
30	6

Puzzle 8 - solution on page: 65

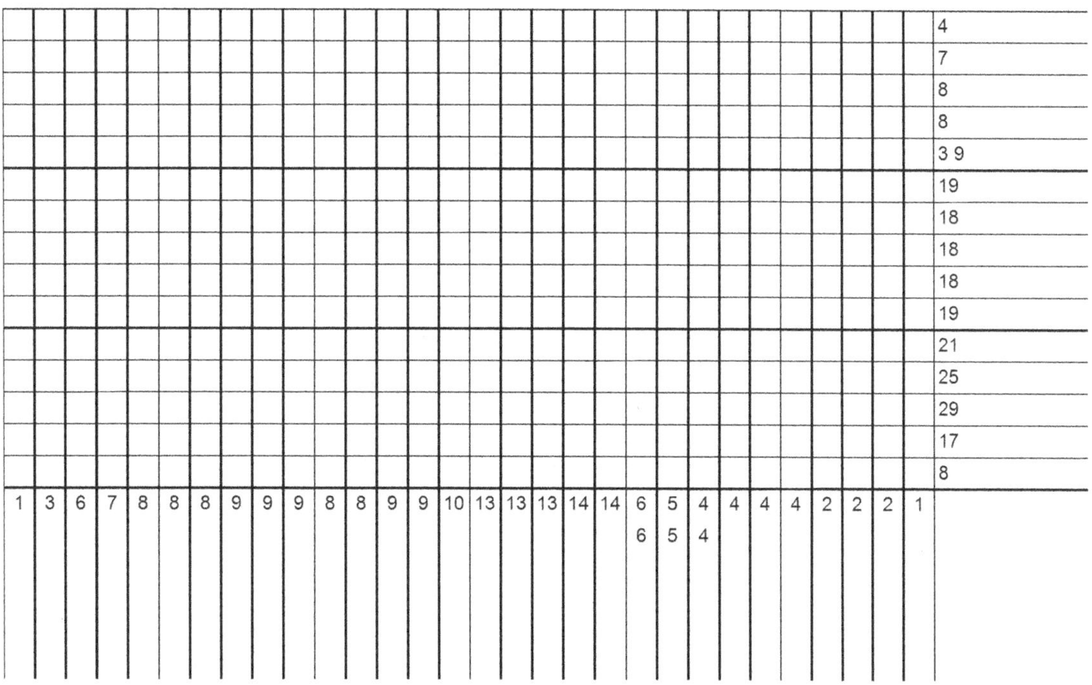

Puzzle 9 - solution on page: 67

Row clues:

2
3
5
7
8
10
16
17
17
17
17
18
12 7
11 4
5 2 1
2 1 2 1
1 1 1 1
2 3 1 1
1

Column clues:

2 | 2 | 3 | 3 3 | 6 2 | 6 | 8 | 11 | 9 1 | 8 1 | 8 | 7 | 6 | 7 | 8 | 8 | 11 | 12 | 9 1 | 13 | 8 1 | 8 | 8 | 7 | 5 | 3 | 2

Puzzle 10 - solution on page: 69

Row clues:

1
1
2 1
7
8
8
7
8
8
17
20
20
20
21
20
20
11 8
9 9
6 3 4
5 2 3
5 2 3
5 2 3
5 2 3
1 2 2 2
1 2 2 2
4 1 2
2 2 2 2
2 1 2
2 2
1

Column clues:

2	4	6	8	12	17	20	24	4	21	18	10	9	9	8	8	7	9	13	16	9	8	9	9	8	5	3	7	5
					2	3		16									1	3		2						1		
								1																				
								2																				

Regular

Puzzle 11 - solution on page: 71

Column clues (left to right):
4 | 15 | 15 | 14 | 12 | 11 | 12 | 13 | 13 | 13 | 13 | 13 | 13 | 14 | 22 | 24 | 21 5 | 20 5 | 19 | 19 | 20 | 21 | 21 | 22 | 22 | 22 | 23 | 23 | 17 3 | 15 4 | 14 3 | 12 3 | 16 3 | 18 3 | 9 6 4 | 4 8 4 | 9 | 7

Row clues (top to bottom):
1
1
2
2
3
3
3
2
1 3
3 2 3
9 4
10 4 2
18 2
21 3
23 7
33
32
29
27
27
27
4 22
3 21
1 20
19 2
18 2
17 2
19 2
18 3
17 3
20
19
18
17
15
14
10
8
5
3
2
2
1
1
2
2
2
1
1

Puzzle 12 - solution on page: 73

Column clues (left to right):

1
2 5
3 9
4 11
4 12
4 12
1 11 12
4 28
35
36
32
40
6 24 5
3 13 6
9 5
5
4
4
1

Row clues (top to bottom):

1
1 1
2 2
2 2
2 2
1 2
2 1 2
4 2 2
4 5
5 5
6 5
6 5
13
13
11
11
11
10
10
9
9
9
8
8
8
8
8
7
8
1 7
2 7
2 6
2 6
9
9
9
9
8
8
7
5
4
3
4
3
3
2
1
1

Puzzle 13 - solution on page: 75

Column clues:

4	7	8 5	10 10	12 4 1	14 6 4 1	36	35	35	3 29	28	27	27	27	27	16 10	14 9	11 10	10 4 5	4 3 4 6	4 3 4 4	3 3 2 3	3 3 2 2	3 3 3 2	3 3 2 3 2	3 7 3 2	2 5 3 2	3 3 1	3 3 1	4 4	2 3

Row clues:

1
2
1
2
2 5
2 4
2 3
2 4
2 3
2 3
3 4
2 6
15
14
12
12
15 2
22
23
16 4
11 3
10 3
11 2
10 2
11
11 1
11 3
12 3
13 2
21
21
20
13
13
16
18
22
23
13 5
10 4
9 3
8 3
8 2
8 1
9
8
6
3
2

Puzzle 14 - solution on page: 77

4 | 7 | 9 | 10 | 13 | 16 | 17 | 17 | 13 | 26 | 31 | 34 | 9 28 | 29 | 28 | 28 | 28 | 26 | 8 15 | 9 12 | 8 5 | 7 5 | 7 4 | 7 3 | 7 3 | 6 4 | 3 2 4 | 2 2 2 | 2 2 3 | 1 3 3 | 3 2 | 1

Row clues (top to bottom):

1
2
4
4
6
7
7
7
8
9
10 2
13 3
15 3
14 10
23
22
17 2
16
13
12
12
11
11
11
11
10
10
10
10
9
9
9
11
12
13
13
14
15 1
20
2 17
3 7 1
2 5 2
2 8
2 5
2
1
1
1
1

uzzle 15 - solution on page: 79

Row clues:

2
4
5
6
5
5
4 1
4 2 10
4 16
4 17
4 17
4 13
4 14
4 13
5 12
12 13
15 17
39
40
39
39
37
37
37
38
37
37
37
37
37
11 25
11 21
10 17
5 4 14
4 3 14
4 3 5 4
4 3 5 4
3 3 4 4
3 4 3 4
3 3 3 4
3 3 4
3 3 4
2 3 4
5 4
5 5
5 4
4

Column clues:

7
10
6 12
9 13
11 15
13 16
5 23
3 27
3 27
1 26
19 2
18
17
16
15
16
16
16
15
16
16
15
16
16
16
20 3
30
30
31
22 4
2 19
6 20
27
27
28
38
38
39
39
25 2
18
14
15
13
4 1 3
4
4

uzzle 16 - solution on page: 81

Row clues:

Row clues
1
2 4
3 6
4 7
12
14
20
20
19
19
20
20
2 20
2 20
3 19
3 13 5
3 14 1
3 14
3 16
5 18
31
32
32
33
33
34
35
35
35
35
35
34
33
32
22 8
6 1 7
4 7
4 7
4 4
3

Column clues:

3	6	11	13	15	6	24	24	16	16	15	15	16	15	15	15	15	15	15	16	16	17	17	18	18	20	23	25	5	37	37	36	35	29	27	26	26	16	14	14	3	2	10	11	10	8	7	6	1
					19	2																						28					3	2			4			11	11							

Hard

Puzzle 17 - solution on page: 83

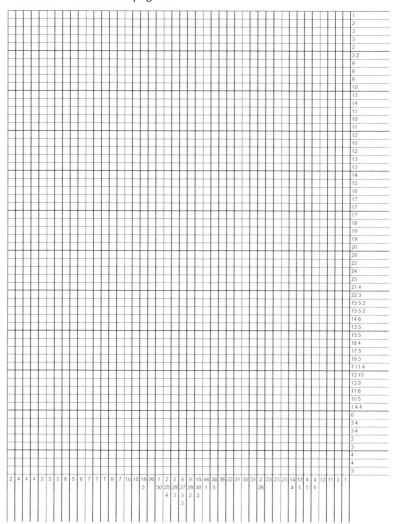

Row clues:

Row	Clue
1	1
2	2
3	3
4	3
5	3
6	3 2
7	9
8	9
9	9
10	10
11	13
12	14
13	11
14	10
15	11
16	12
17	10
18	12
19	13
20	13
21	14
22	15
23	16
24	17
25	17
26	17
27	18
28	19
29	19
30	20
31	20
32	22
33	24
34	25
35	21 4
36	22 3
37	15 5 2
38	15 5 2
39	14 6
40	13 5
41	15 5
42	16 4
43	17 3
44	18 3
45	7 11 4
46	12 10
47	13 9
48	11 6
49	10 5
50	1 4 4
51	6
52	3 4
53	3 4
54	2
55	3
56	4
57	4
58	3

Column clues:

Column	Clue
1	2
2	4
3	4
4	4
5	5
6	5
7	5
8	6
9	5
10	6
11	7
12	7
13	7
14	8
15	7
16	10
17	15
18	18 3
19	26
20	1 30
21	2 25 4
22	2 29 3
23	4 27 3 3
24	9 29 2
25	10 30 2
26	44 1
27	38 5
28	38
29	32
30	31
31	30
32	31
33	2 26
34	23
35	23
36	21
37	14 4
38	12 5
39	4 5
40	4 5
41	12
42	11
43	2
44	1

Puzzle 18 - solution on page: 85

Row clues:

4
6 8
21
18
17
17
15
15
15
15
16
17
18
9 21
42
44
45
45
46
47
47
48
48
48
3 45
2 45
2 44
1 44
1 44
2 43
10 33
6 32
5 5 23
4 5 20
4 5 11
3 4 11
4 4 11
4 5 5 4
4 4 4 4
3 3 4 4
3 3 4 3
3 3 8
3 5 4 3
3 6 3 3
4 4 4 4
4 3 5
5 3 5
5 4
6
6
4

Column clues:

4
7 4
5 2 11
4 1 12
5 20
21 2
20
19
18
17
16
16
16
17 1
25
28
29
31
22 4
19 3
19 3
19 3
20 1
20
19
20
20
20
20
20
20
20
20
25 1
33
37
1 38
2 31 5
3 26 1 4
5 35 3
45 2
46
39 3
35 2
32 2
30 1
28
27
26
24
20
16
14
13
12
5
2
1
1

Puzzle 19 - solution on page: 87

Row clues (top to bottom):

2
3
4
4
4
4
4
4
4
5
5
4
4 11
5 15
23
24
26
28
37 2
45
46
47
47
47
47
46
46
45
45
10 35
8 19 10
7 17 5 2
5 15 5
5 12 4
6 11
6 8
7 7
8 8
4 4 8
3 3 4 5
3 4 5 4
4 3 4 4
4 3 4
4 3 4
4 3 3
1 3 4
4 4
4 6
7
6
1

Column clues (left to right):

4 | 9 | 10 | 10 | 10 | 6 | 7 | 14 | 14 | 14 | 14 | 17 5 | 27 | 30 | 31 | 26 5 | 27 4 | 20 5 4 | 20 5 2 | 19 4 | 18 2 | 17 | 18 8 | 19 9 | 19 11 | 20 8 2 | 27 | 25 | 25 | 27 | 28 | 30 | 19 8 | 18 7 | 18 5 | 17 4 | 16 3 | 16 3 | 15 4 | 15 2 | 14 | 13 | 12 | 12 | 11 | 11 | 12 | 13 | 14 | 15 | 15 | 15 | 14 | 10 | 6 | 4 | 2

Puzzle 20 - solution on page: 89

Row clues (top to bottom):

6
1 8
2 9 12
2 15 16
26 20
48
46
45
46
37 4
37
36
35
35
7 7 19
6 6 19
7 5 17
6 4 15
6 3 7 6
6 3 4 5
5 3 4 5
5 3 4 5
4 3 3 5
3 3 3 5
3 3 3 5
2 4 2 5
2 3 2 4
2 3 3 3
2 2 3 3
2 2 3 3
2 6 4
2 4 3
1 2 3
2 4
2 4
2

Column clues (left to right):

2
6
11
5
5
4
4
2 6
2 7
2 10
1 13
15
14
14
12
12
13
14
15
16
18
24
25
12 8
11 4
12 3
13 3
13 5
13 5
13 2
14 2
15 1 4
26
25
21
16
14
14
13
15
16
19
20
22
10 10
9 6
9 4
8 4
8 4
8 4
8 5
8 3
9 3
9 4
8 4
4 2 4
4 3
2 1
2

Puzzle 21 - solution on page: 91

Row clues (top to bottom):

1
2
3
3 1
3 2
6
8
8
6
9
9
9
11
11
15
16
17
19
21
25
29
30
30
30
30
30
31
31
30
19 10
18 1 1
17
16
17
17
17
18
18
18
19
21
22
23
22
19
18
17
16
16
15
15
14
13
12
10
8
4

Column clues (left to right):

	1	2	4	5	6	9	13	18	21	26	31	34	1 37	49	55	56	55	52	54	52	50	47	26 15	19 11	17 6	16	15	16	15	14	14	12	11	11	12	11	10	9	8	2

Puzzle 22 - solution on page: 93

Row clues:

Row clues
1
1 1
2 1
3 3
5 3
12
14
14
15
15
15
16
16
18
18
19
19
19
20
21
19
21
26
28
30
31
32
33
33
34
34
35
35
36
37
36
37
36
36
10 23
8 12 5
7 8 5
7 8 5
5 8 5
5 7 5
4 6 5
4 5 4
4 4 4
3 4 4
4 6 4
4 6 4
3 7 4
3 8 4
4 10 3
4 5 5 4
2 5 4 4
5 2 4
3 5
4

Column clues:

Column clues
3
6
7
8
5 2
6
6
8
10
11
11
12
14
15
15
15
16
15
16
16
17
18
18 4
19 9
37
37
36
34
27 6
27 5
27 4
27 4
26 3
28
30
34
35
37
51
55
54
55
41 5
35 3
34 2
20 13
17
15
14
12
4

Solutions

Solution for Puzzle 1 on page 7

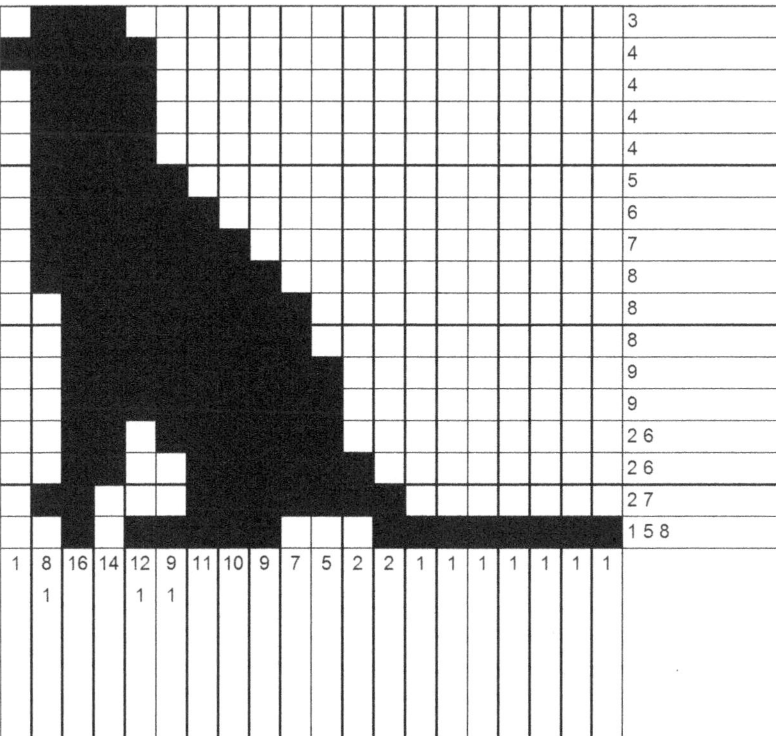

Solution for Puzzle 2 on page 7

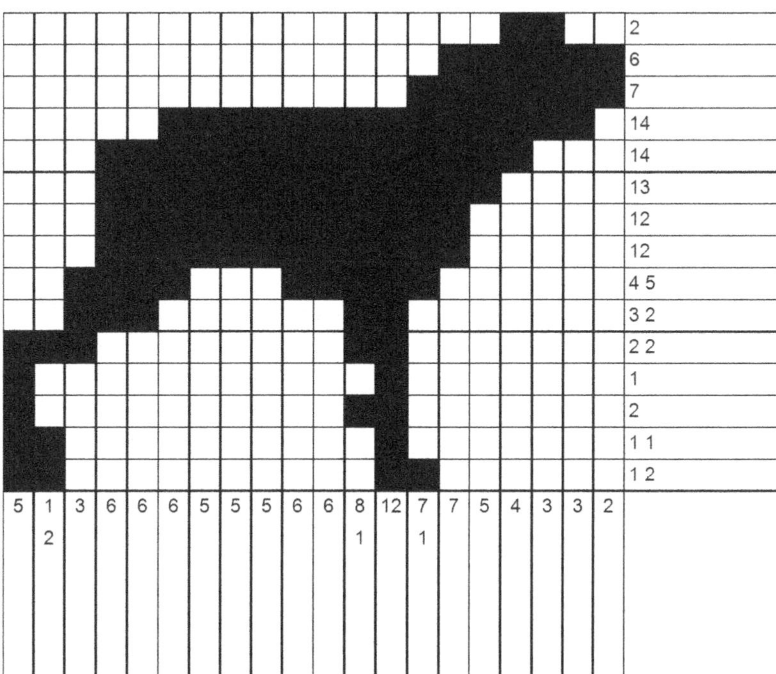

Solution for Puzzle 3 on page 9

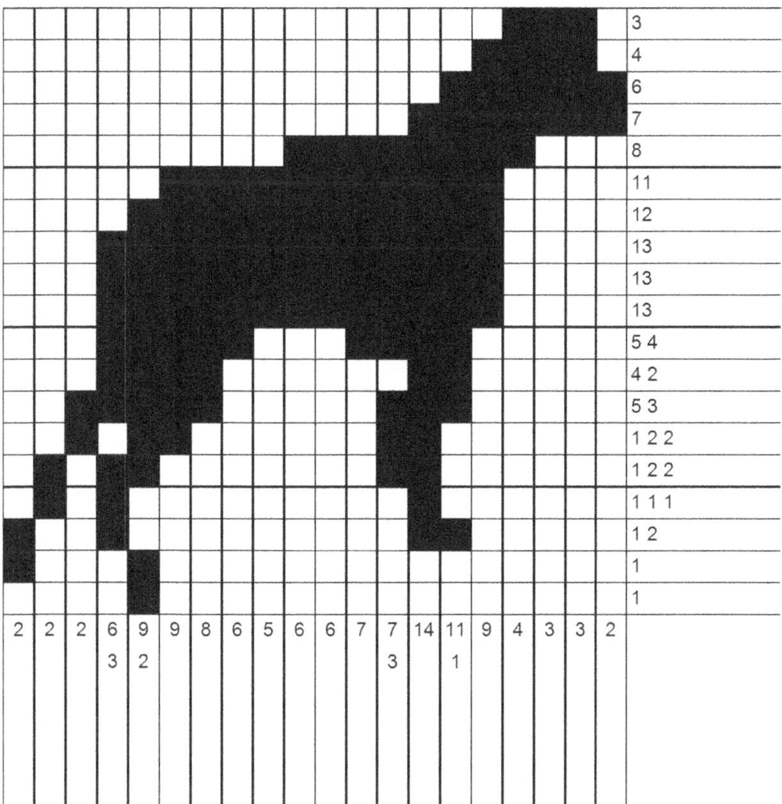

Solution for Puzzle 4 on page 9

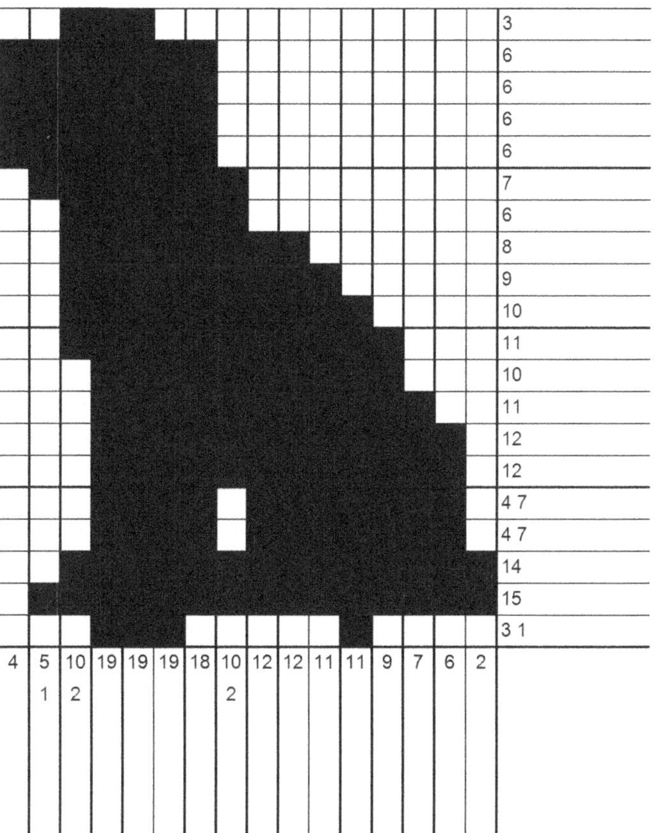

Solution for Puzzle 5 on page 13

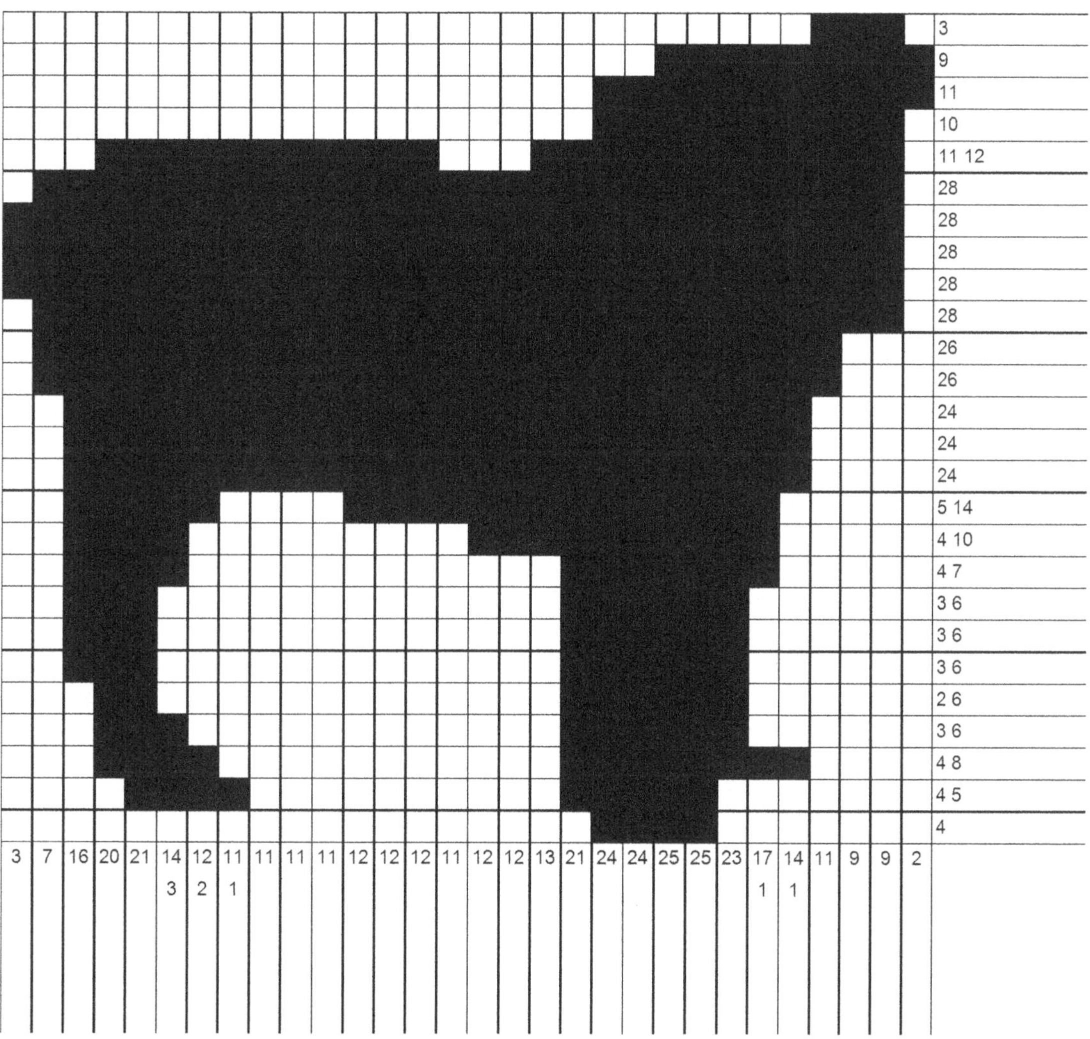

Solution for Puzzle 6 on page 15

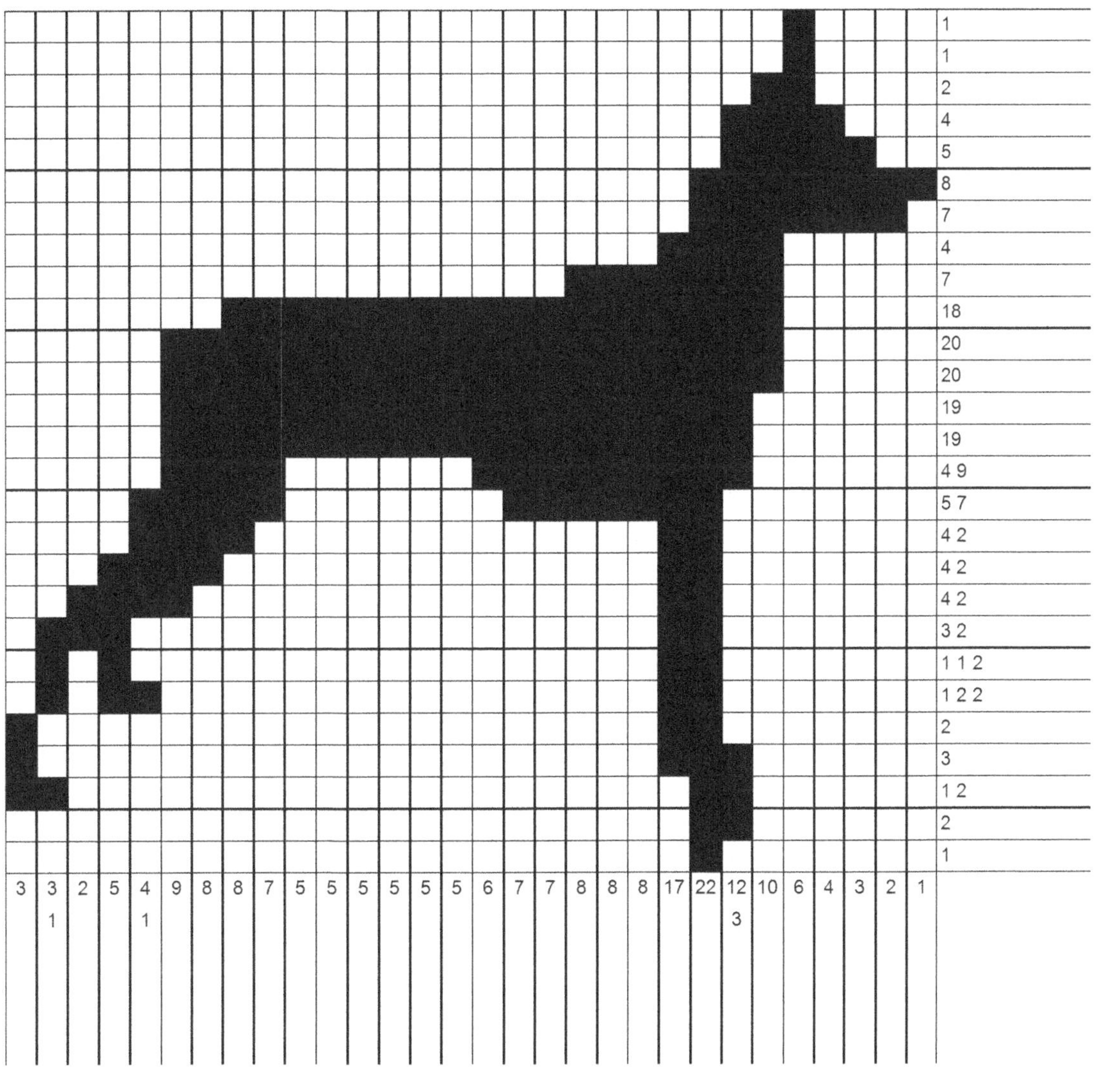

Solution for Puzzle 7 on page 17

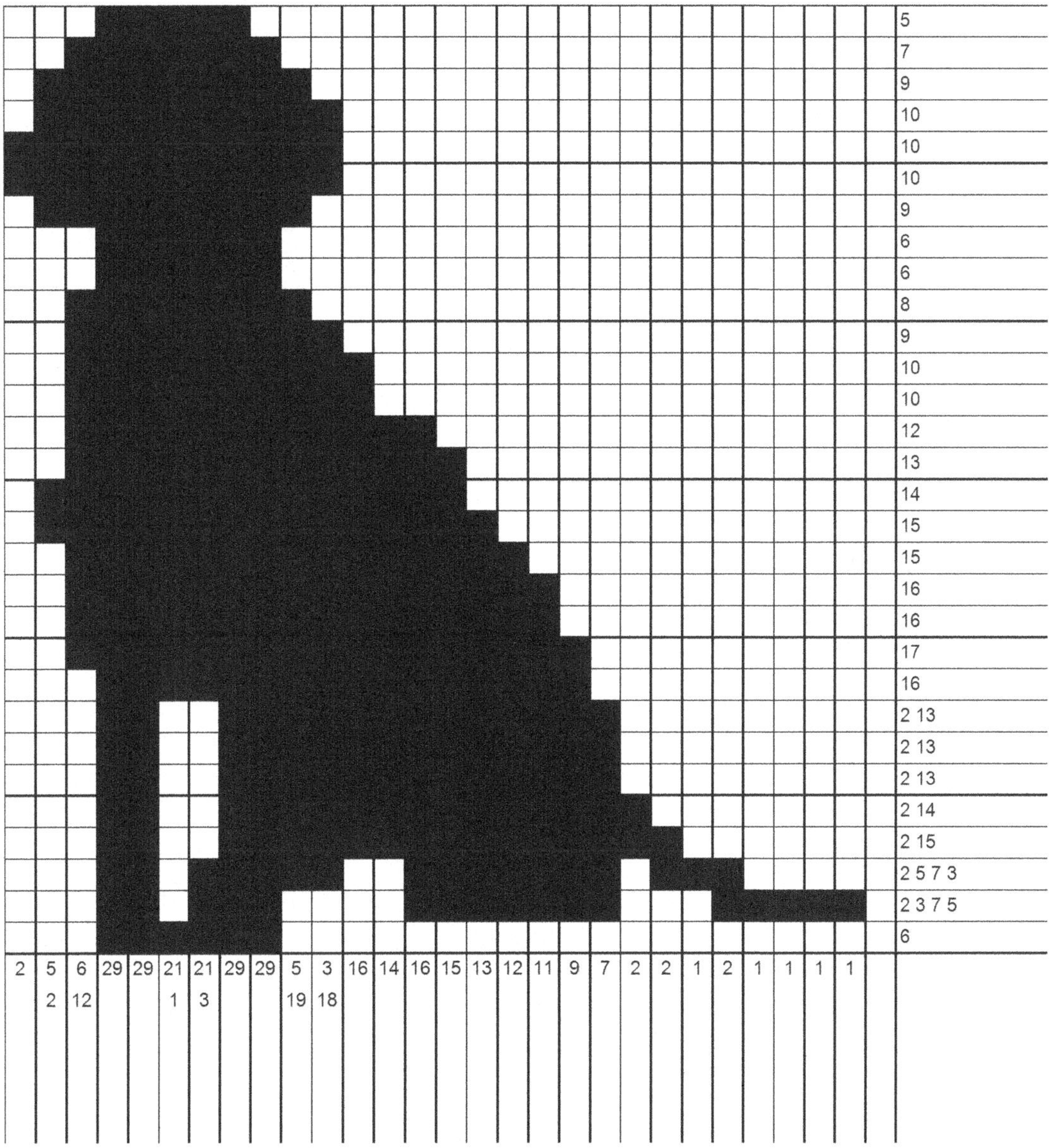

Row clues:

Row	Clue
1	5
2	7
3	9
4	10
5	10
6	10
7	9
8	6
9	6
10	8
11	9
12	10
13	10
14	12
15	13
16	14
17	15
18	15
19	16
20	16
21	17
22	16
23	2 13
24	2 13
25	2 13
26	2 14
27	2 15
28	2 5 7 3
29	2 3 7 5
30	6

Column clues:

2	5	6	29	29	21	21	29	29	5	3	16	14	16	15	13	12	11	9	7	2	2	1	2	1	1	1	1	
	2	12			1	3			19	18																		

Solution for Puzzle 8 on page 19

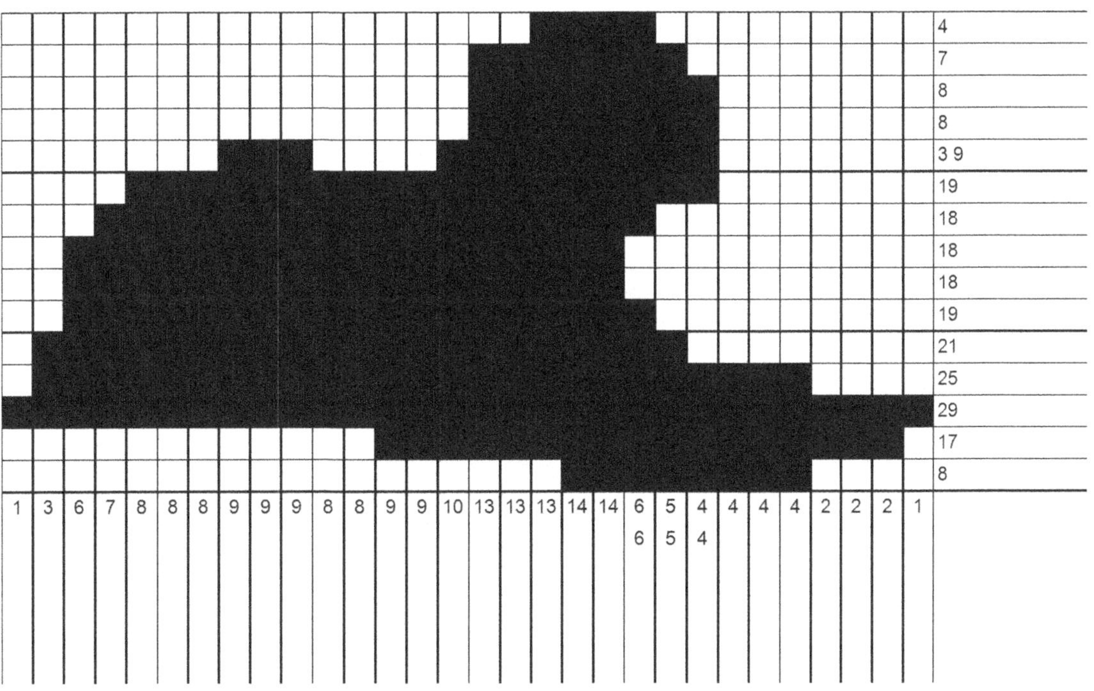

Solution for Puzzle 9 on page 21

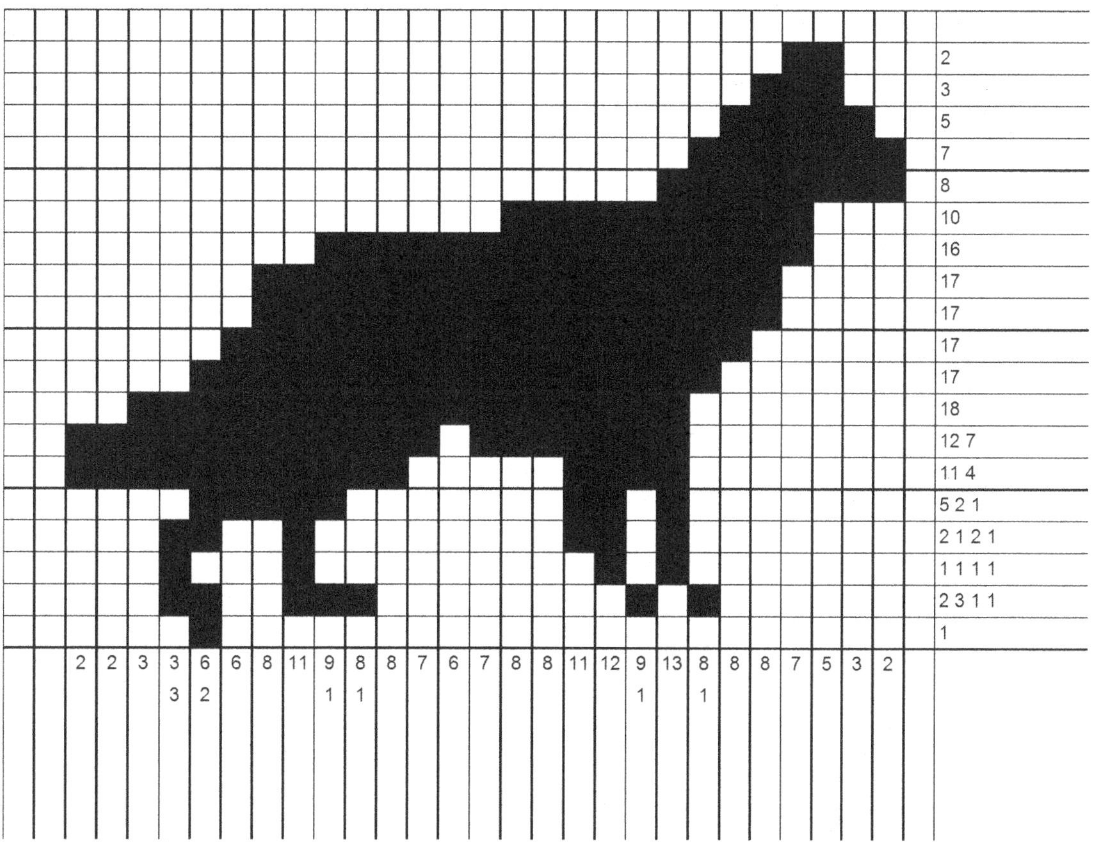

Solution for Puzzle 10 on page 23

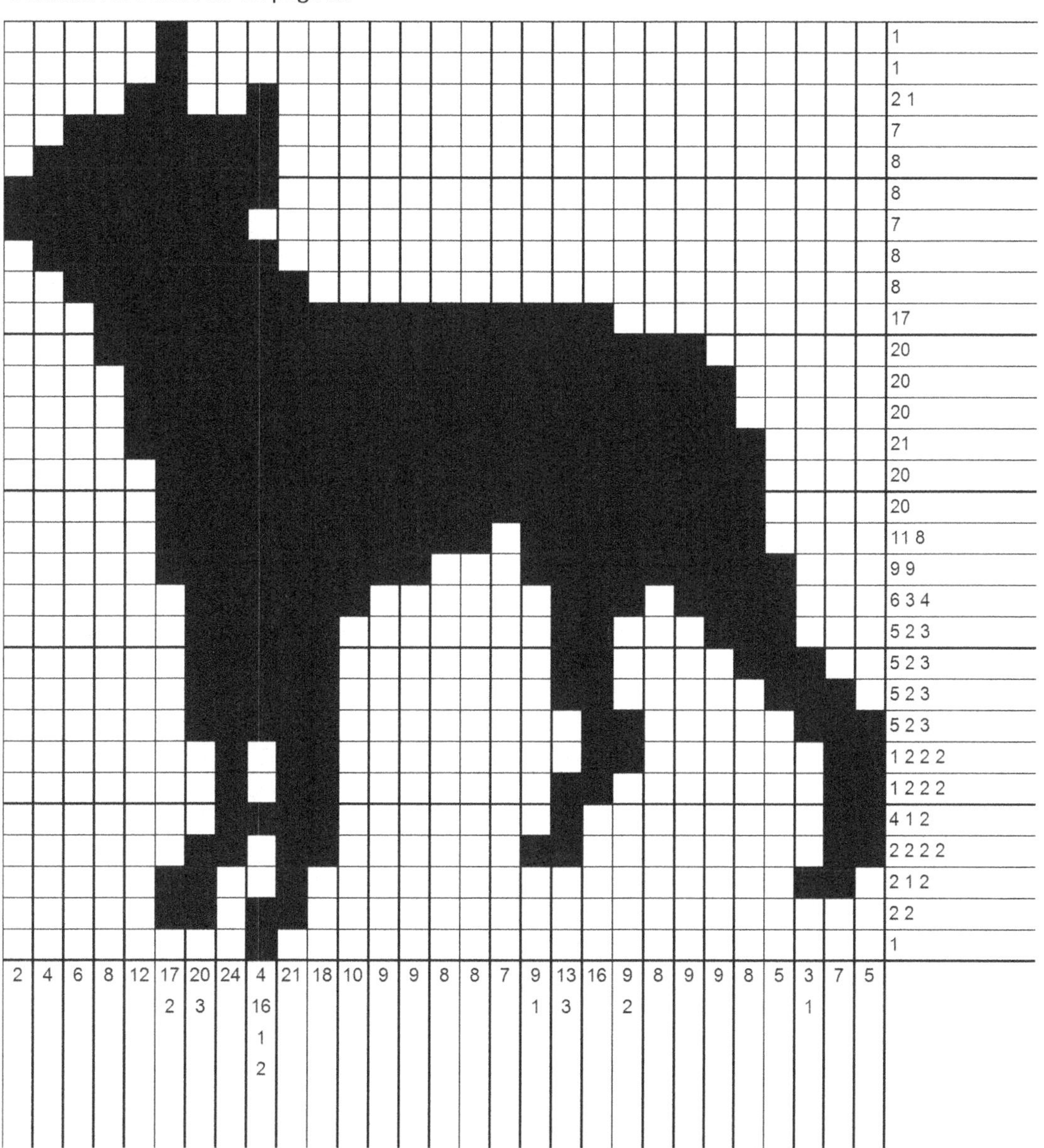

Solution for Puzzle 11 on page 27

Column clues: 4 | 15 | 15 | 14 | 12 | 11 | 12 | 13 | 13 | 13 | 13 | 13 | 13 | 14 | 22 | 24 | 21 5 | 20 5 | 19 | 19 | 20 | 21 | 21 | 22 | 22 | 22 | 23 | 23 | 17 3 | 15 4 | 14 3 | 12 3 | 16 3 | 18 3 | 9 6 4 | 4 8 4 | 9 | 7

Row clues:
1
1
2
2
3
3
3
2
1 3
3 2 3
9 4
10 4 2
18 2
21 3
23 7
33
32
29
27
27
27
4 22
3 21
1 20
19 2
18 2
17 2
19 2
18 3
17 3
20
19
18
17
15
14
10
8
5
3
2
2
1
1
2
2
2
1
1

Solution for Puzzle 12 on page 29

Column clues: 1 | 2 5 | 3 9 | 4 11 | 4 12 | 4 12 | 1 11 12 | 4 28 | 35 | 36 | 32 | 40 | 6 24 5 | 3 13 6 | 9 5 | 5 | 4 | 4 | 1

Row clues:
1
1 1
2 2
2 2
2 2
1 2
2 1 2
4 2 2
4 5
5 5
6 5
6 5
13
13
11
11
11
10
10
9
9
9
8
8
8
8
8
7
8
1 7
2 7
2 6
2 6
9
9
9
9
8
8
7
5
4
3
4
3
3
2
1
1

Solution for Puzzle 13 on page 31

Column clues: 4 | 7 | 8 5 | 10 10 | 12 4 1 | 14 6 4 1 | 36 | 35 | 35 | 3 29 | 28 | 27 | 27 | 27 | 27 | 16 10 | 14 9 | 11 10 | 10 4 5 | 4 3 4 6 | 4 3 4 4 | 3 3 2 3 | 3 3 2 2 | 3 3 3 2 | 3 3 2 3 2 | 3 7 3 2 | 2 5 3 2 | 3 3 1 | 3 3 1 | 4 4 | 2 3

Row clues: 1 | 2 | 1 | 2 | 2 5 | 2 4 | 2 3 | 2 4 | 2 3 | 2 3 | 3 4 | 2 6 | 15 | 14 | 12 | 12 | 15 2 | 22 | 23 | 16 4 | 11 3 | 10 3 | 11 2 | 10 2 | 11 | 11 1 | 11 3 | 12 3 | 13 2 | 21 | 21 | 20 | 13 | 13 | 16 | 18 | 22 | 23 | 13 5 | 10 4 | 9 3 | 8 3 | 8 2 | 8 1 | 9 | 8 | 6 | 3 | 2

Solution for Puzzle 14 on page 33

Column clues: 4 | 7 | 9 | 10 | 13 | 16 | 17 | 17 | 13 | 26 | 31 | 34 | 9 28 | 29 | 28 | 28 | 28 | 26 | 8 15 | 9 12 | 8 5 | 7 5 | 7 4 | 7 3 | 7 3 | 6 4 | 3 2 4 | 2 2 2 | 2 2 3 | 1 3 3 | 3 2 | 1

Row clues: 1 | 2 | 4 | 4 | 6 | 7 | 7 | 7 | 8 | 9 | 10 2 | 13 3 | 15 3 | 14 10 | 23 | 22 | 17 2 | 16 | 13 | 12 | 12 | 11 | 11 | 11 | 11 | 10 | 10 | 10 | 10 | 9 | 9 | 9 | 11 | 12 | 13 | 13 | 14 | 15 1 | 20 | 2 17 | 3 7 1 | 2 5 2 | 2 8 | 2 5 | 2 | 1 | 1 | 1 | 1

lution for Puzzle 15 on page 35

lution for Puzzle 16 on page 37

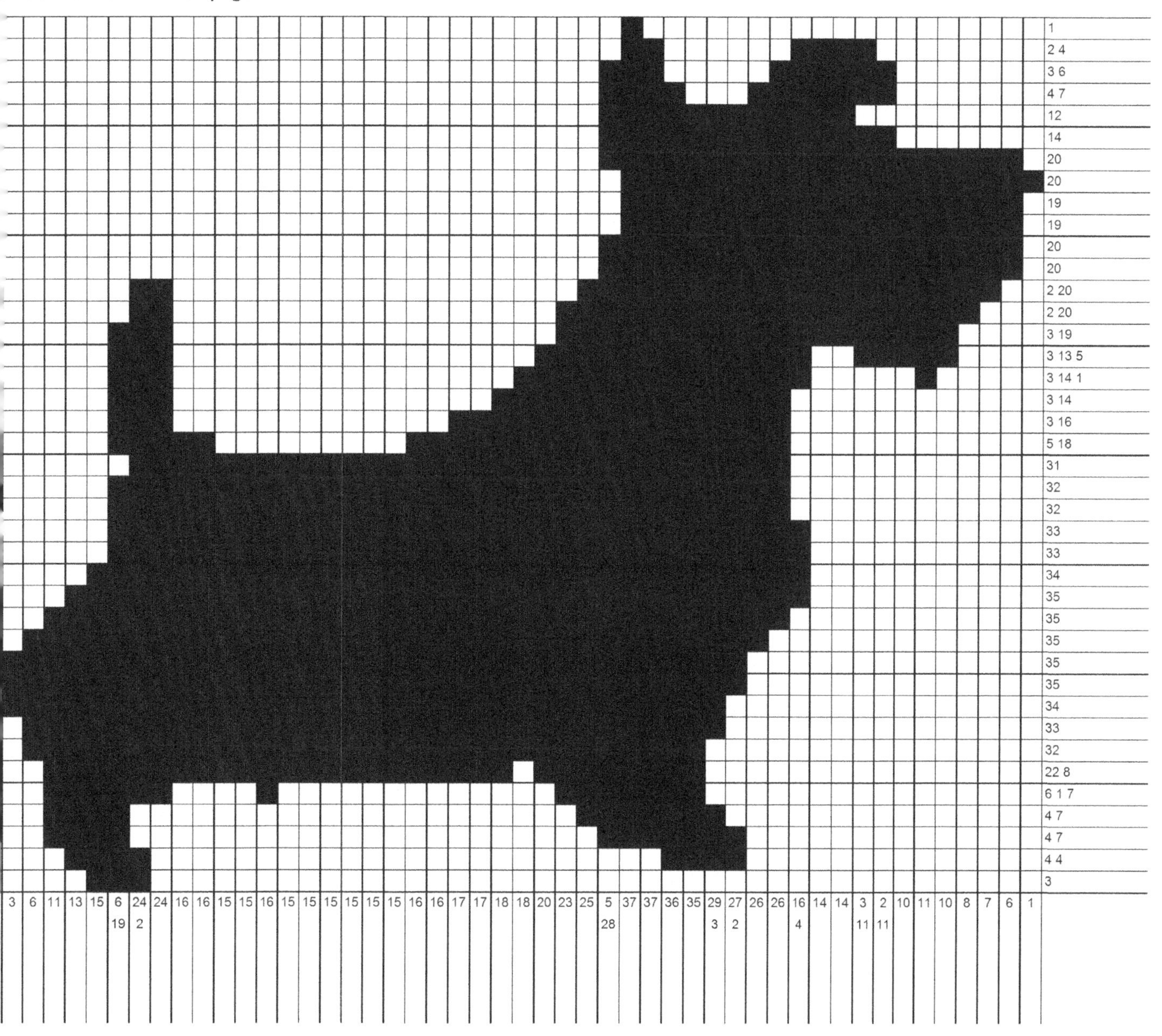

Solution for Puzzle 17 on page 41

Solution for Puzzle 18 on page 43

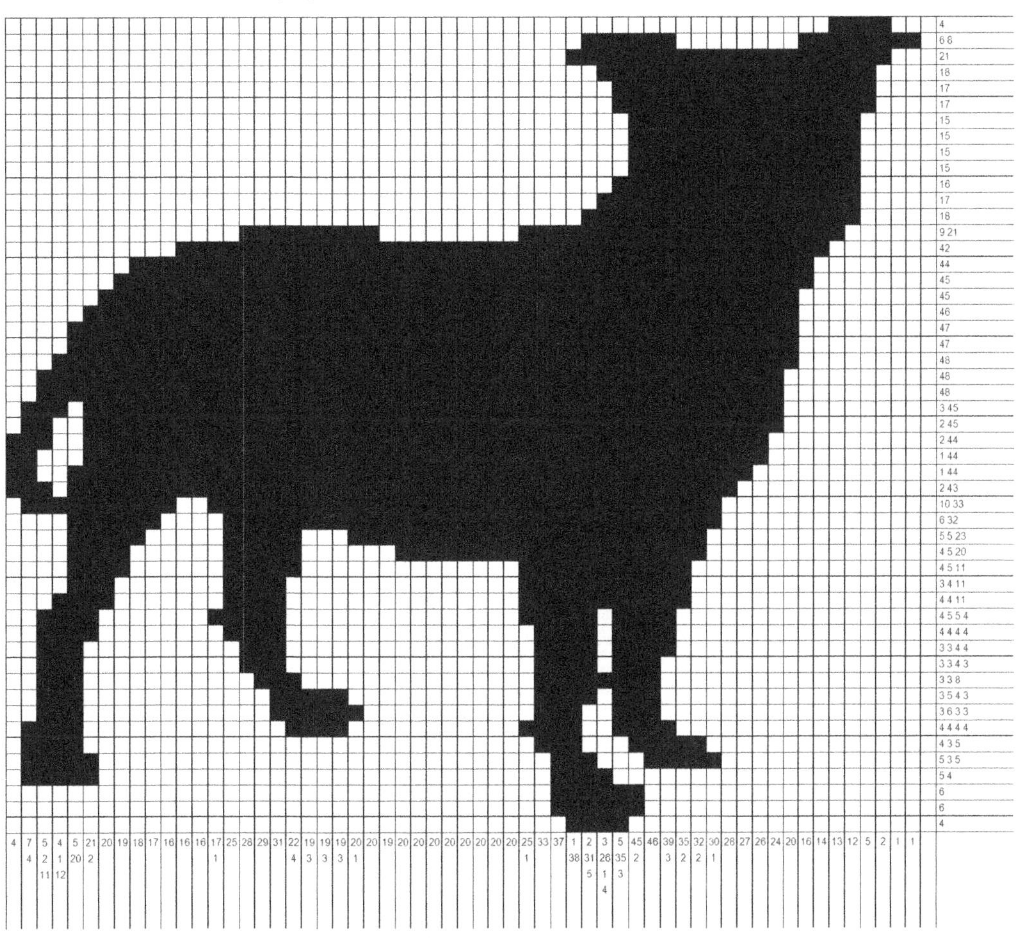

Solution for Puzzle 19 on page 45

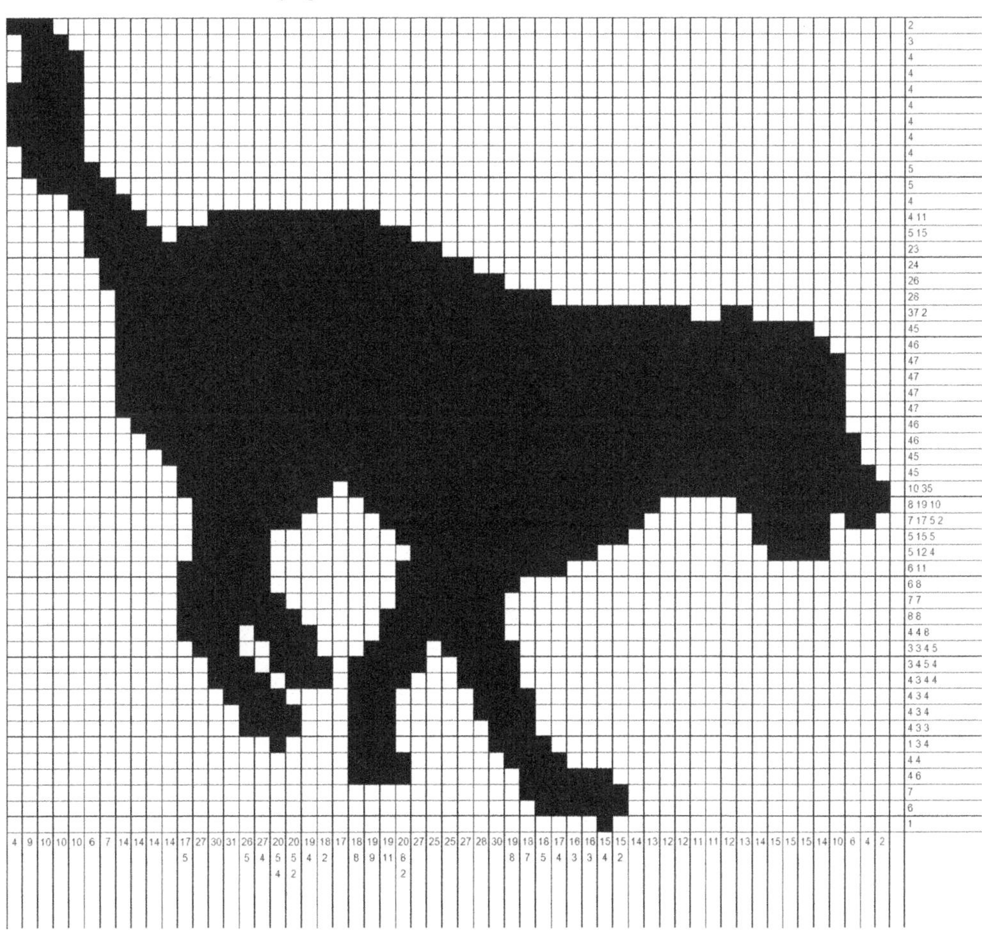

Solution for Puzzle 20 on page 47

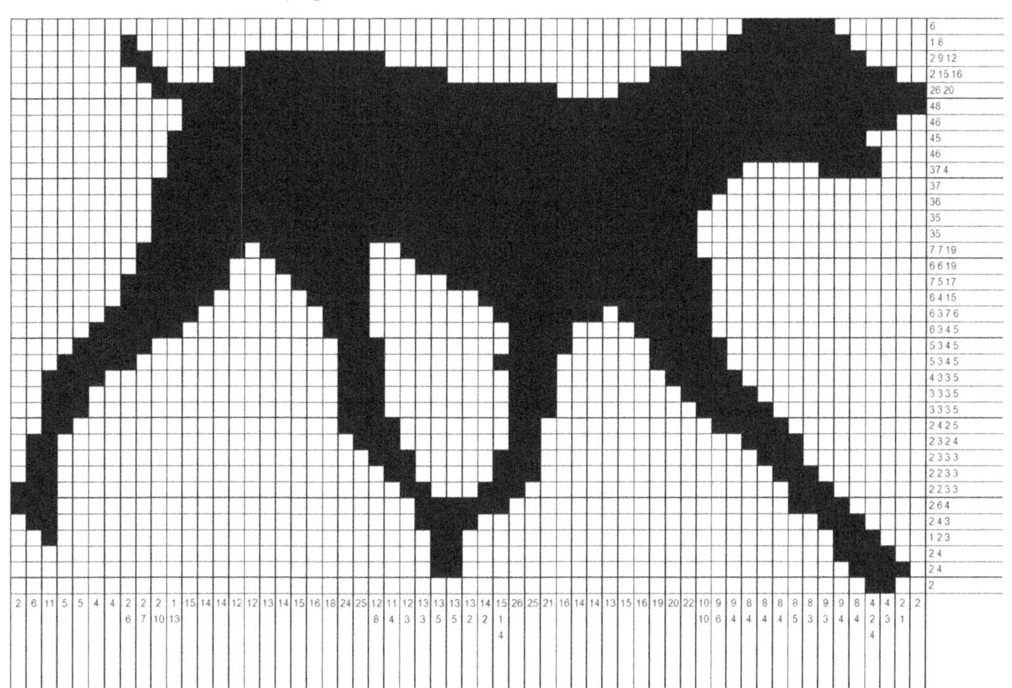

Solution for Puzzle 21 on page 49

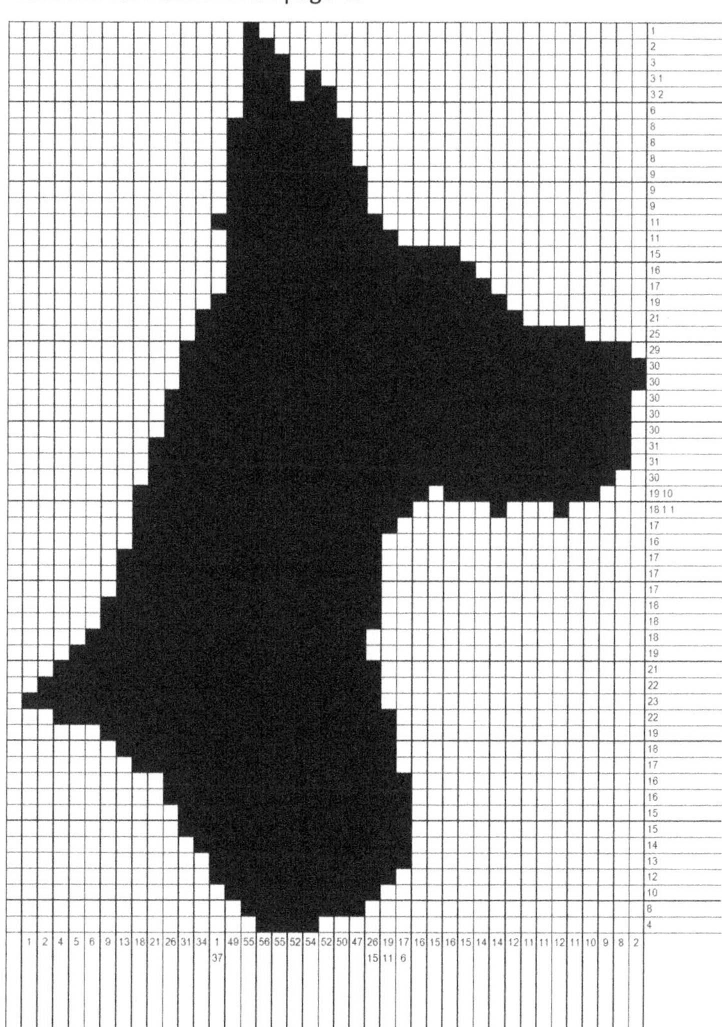

Solution for Puzzle 22 on page 51

Did you enjoy this coloring book? Feel free to leave a review at Amazon.com or any other online bookstore where you bought this book.

Please send suggestions, comments or complaints directly to us at:

Email: feedback@quipoppe.com.

Find more Quipoppe Publications books at Amazon.com:

https://www.amazon.com/author/quipoppe

Find out the latest news and announcements from Quipoppe Publications:

http://www.quipoppe.com

On our Facebook page you will find:

- The latest news and announcements
- Discussions with other fans AND fast response from us to your questions and comments
- Contests
- Free downloadable coloring books
- A place to show off your coloring art

https://www.facebook.com/Quipoppe

Made in the USA
Monee, IL
22 January 2021